"We live in a world filled with psychic phenomena pointing to the survival of the human mind and individual consciousness, which continues to live on after bodily death. In certain situations it can make its presence known to us. There are no ultimate answers, and most of us have had our doubts However, there is compelling evidence for what men and women have believed for thousands of years----there is life *after* life."

----from a chapter written for this edition

AuthorHouse™
1663 Liberty Drive
Bloomington, IN 47403
www.authorhouse.com
Phone: 1-800-839-8640

Published by AuthorHouse   09/13/2012

ISBN: 978-1-4772-4106-6 (sc)
ISBN: 978-1-4772-4105-9 (e)

Library of Congress Control Number: 2012912290

INQUIRY?

A MODERN STUDY OF JESUS
AND PSYCHIC PHENOMENA

Michael   Zyvant

authorHOUSE®

"What we call life is a journey to death. What we call death is the gateway to life."
----Anonymous

Contents

Introduction

I'm not an atheist or an evangelist. I didn't write *Inquiry* to prove something or to uphold a particular point of view. Just consider my book an information manual, and apply it as you see fit.

My wish is that reading these pages will make a *worthwhile* difference in the lives of people----especially my wife, our children, and our grandchildren.

Gospels

Origin

Oral history is unwritten information provided by an eyewitness that has been a part of an historic event. Toward the end of the first century, the oral history concerning Jesus was decreasing, because his apostles and other eyewitnesses were dying. Since the oral history lacked written documentation, it was very easy for disagreements regarding the interpretation to occur.

These factors made it necessary to gather writings that accurately portrayed the life and teachings of Jesus. This resulted in the Gospels of Matthew, Mark, Luke, and John (the first four books of the New Testament).

Text

All the Gospels were written in Greek. The word *gospel* was originally derived as a translation for the Greek word *evangelion*, meaning "good news." The name Jesus is derived from a Greek translation for the Hebrew name of Joshua. Christ is a derivative of a Greek translation of the Hebrew word for Messiah. It is generally believed the Gospels were written in the first century.

Authority

The unique authority of the Gospels in portraying Jesus' life and teachings has been accepted by Christians and their churches as authentic and inspired Holy Scriptures. Therefore, the Gospels were the source for the story of Jesus in this book.

Birth and Childhood

Mary

God sent the angel Gabriel to Mary, a virgin. She
was engaged to a man named Joseph. Gabriel told
Mary that she had been favored by God. Then he
told her she would conceive a baby boy through the
power of the Holy Spirit, and he would be called the
Son of God. (Christian theologians understand God
as a unity of three or Trinity: Father, Son, and Holy

Spirit.) Mary agreed to do whatever God wanted, and Gabriel departed.

Joseph

Mary was engaged to Joseph when she was found to be pregnant by the Holy Spirit. Joseph wanted to break the engagement. However, Joseph brought Mary home to be his wife after her pregnancy had been explained to him in a dream.

Source

Some believe the accounts of the Virginal Conception are historical, based on reports from Mary and Joseph. Others believe they are theological interpretations. Whatever the source, the story of the Virginal Conception provides the basis for the traditional belief in the divine origin of Jesus' birth.

POSTSCRIPT. The following narratives of Matthew and Luke contain the only birth and childhood stories of Jesus that are found in the Gospels.

Matthew's Narrative

Astrologers Visit Jerusalem

During the reign of King Herod, Jesus was born in Bethlehem, a town in Judea (part of the Roman-ruled region of Palestine). After Jesus' birth, some astrologers from eastern countries arrived in Jerusalem. The astrologers were looking for the newborn King of the Jews. They had seen his star and had come to worship him.

POSTSCRIPT. The name *Magi* has been used to describe the astrologers that came to Jerusalem looking for the newborn King of the Jews. The Magi (singular Magus) were a priestly order from ancient Persia. Considered *wise men*, the Magi were well-versed in astrology.

Star of Bethlehem

The star the Magi saw is traditionally called the Star of Bethlehem. A possible explanation for the appearance of the star is the conjunction of the planets Mars, Jupiter, and Saturn. This occurs when the positions of these planets are aligned. Modern planetariums are now able to simulate this planetary configuration from the remote past.

King Herod Sends the Magi to Bethlehem

King Herod was very troubled when he heard the Magi were searching for a newborn King of the Jews. So Herod questioned religious leaders. They told him that it was prophesied the Messiah (the expected king and savior of the Jews) would be born in Bethlehem.

Herod met with the Magi. He found out from them the time the star appeared, and he instructed them to search for the child in Bethlehem. Herod also told the Magi to come back and report to him when they found the child, because he wanted to go and worship him too.

Visit of the Magi

After their meeting with Herod, the Magi left Jerusalem. The star appeared to them again, and they found the child with his mother, Mary. The Magi paid homage to the child and presented him with gifts of gold, frankincense, and myrrh.

POSTSCRIPT. Tradition has elaborated on the Gospels' account of the Magi as follows: (1) The Magi presented three gifts to the infant Jesus, and their number was set at three. (2) They've been called kings and named Gaspar, Melchior, and Balthazar.

Flight to Egypt

The Magi were warned in a dream not to return to Jerusalem and report to King Herod. So they used a different route to travel home. After the Magi left, Joseph was instructed in a dream to flee to Egypt with his family, because Herod was going to try and kill the child. Joseph immediately took the child Jesus and Mary to Egypt.

POSTSCRIPT. Altered states of consciousness, like sleeping and dreaming, have been shown to aid the flow of psychic information to the mind. A notable example of this is Joseph's dream warning him that

King Herod would try to kill the child Jesus.

Edgar Cayce (1877-1945) is another example of this psychic phenomenon. While in a deep sleeping state, Cayce provided diagnoses and prescriptions for his patients that cured many diseases (some considered hopeless). The source and nature of Edgar Cayce's amazing ability remains a mystery.

King Herod Slaughters Babies

When the Magi didn't return, Herod realized they had tricked him. Earlier, the Magi told Herod the star had first appeared to them two years before. In keeping with this information, Herod gave orders to kill all the boys in Bethlehem and the surrounding area that were two years old or younger.

After Herod died, Joseph left Egypt. He took the

infant Jesus and Mary to Galilee (a province of Roman-ruled Palestine). They lived in the town of Nazareth.

POSTSCRIPT. At this time, there is no historical reference to corroborate a slaughter of babies by Herod. But history does record Herod's cruelty. He executed three of his sons and one of his ten wives. Of course, any historical reference to the killing of children by Herod may have been destroyed or lost.

King Herod and History

Historically, King Herod is known as Herod the Great. Herod (a Jew) was a friend of Marc Antony, who made him King of Judea. A mere protégé of the Romans, Herod ruled in their interest. Herod was hated by the people. So he tried to appease them by his public observance of the Mosaic law and his magnificent reconstruction of Solomon's Temple in Jerusalem.

Eventually, excessive taxation and Roman brutality made the Jewish people more resistant to Roman authority. A fanatical Jewish sect, called Zealots, turned to assassination and violence against the Romans and their Jewish followers. Meanwhile, Herod was ready to kill any rival king or potential Messiah, whose existence could encourage a desperate people to revolt.

POSTSCRIPT. In 70 A.D., the Roman legions of Titus destroyed Solomon's Temple (rebuilt by Herod) while crushing a major Jewish rebellion.

Luke's Narrative

The Birth of Jesus

The Roman Emperor Augustus ordered a census. Everyone registered in his own city. Joseph, who was from Nazareth in Galilee, was a descendant of King David. So he went to Bethlehem in Judea, where David was born, to register for the census.

Joseph took Mary with him. She was promised in marriage to Joseph, and she was pregnant. After they arrived in Bethlehem, Mary gave birth to a son. She wrapped him in a blanket and laid him in a manger (feeding trough), because there was no room for them in the village inn.

POSTSCRIPT. Augustus was the first Roman emperor. He ruled from 27 B.C. to 14 A.D. History credits

Augustus with introducing a census to improve the system of taxation.

The Angel and the Shepherds

The night that Mary gave birth, there were some shepherds in nearby fields caring for their sheep. An angel appeared to the shepherds. He told the shepherds that the Savior (Messiah) had been born in Bethlehem, and this was good news for everyone. The angel also told the shepherds they would find the newborn baby wrapped in a blanket and lying in a manger.

POSTSCRIPT. The term *angel* is derived from the Greek word *angelos*, meaning "messenger." It appears to have been used by the authors of the Gospels to describe any one they believed delivered a message from God----in human form.

Visit of the Shepherds

The shepherds went to Bethlehem where they found Joseph, Mary, and the newborn baby. The baby was lying in a manger. After seeing the baby, the shepherds told everyone what the angel had said about the infant. Praising God, the shepherds went back to their fields and flocks.

The Child Jesus

At the circumcision ceremony, the child was named Jesus. In accordance with the Mosaic law, Joseph and Mary brought the newborn child to the Temple in Jerusalem to present him to God. When Joseph and Mary had fulfilled all the requirements of the Law, they returned home to the town of Nazareth in Galilee, where the child Jesus grew into boyhood.

The Boy Jesus

When Jesus was twelve years of age, he went to Jerusalem with his parents for the Passover celebration. While returning home to Nazareth, Joseph and Mary noticed that Jesus was not with them. They went back to Jerusalem. After three days, they found Jesus in the Temple. He was sitting with the teachers and amazing everyone with his understanding.

POSTSCRIPT. There is an eighteen year gap between Jesus' visit to the Temple at age twelve and the beginning of his ministry, when he was about thirty years old. The Gospels do not cover that period of Jesus' life.

Summary Analysis

Birth Year

The birth year of Jesus Christ was determined to be 1 A.D. by early Christians. The AD is from Latin *anno Domini,* meaning "the year of the Lord." The year before 1 A.D. was designated 1 B.C. (before Christ). Jesus was born during the reign of King Herod. Modern chronology places Herod's death at 4 B.C. This would make the birth year previously adopted for Jesus wrong by at least four years.

Birthday

It was not until the fourth century that December 25 (Christmas) was chosen to celebrate the birthday of Jesus. This day was selected to counter pagan festivals linked to the Winter Solstice, celebrated in Rome on December 25. January 6 (a date also associated with the Winter Solstice) was the day preferred to celebrate Jesus' birth in the East.

Eventually, the East added Christmas (December 25) as a religious holiday. The West added Epiphany (January 6), which celebrates the Magi's visit to the infant Jesus. In the West, festivals and celebrations highlighted the Twelve Days (December 25-January 6).

Present-day commercial development of Christmas has effectively pushed back the Christmas festivities of the Twelve Days to the period before Christmas.

Closing Thoughts

Accounts of the Virginal Conception, the Magi, and the Shepherds recognize the divinity of Jesus. The power of these stories comes from the energy put into them by prayer, by ceremony, and enthusiastic expression. Throughout the history of Christianity, that power shows itself to be awesome.

Ministry

Baptism of Jesus

The Gospels record Jesus' baptism by John the
Baptist. These accounts provide the basis for the
special significance attached to it. The sacrament of
baptism is derived from this event.

Temptation of Jesus

After being baptized, Jesus went into the

seclusion and solitude of the desert for forty days and fasted. Jesus' virtue was tested by the temptations of Satan, from the lure of food to the prospect of worldwide power. Satan was unable to tempt Jesus, and he left him.

POSTSCRIPT. Some view Satan's temptation of Jesus as one of the symbolic events included in the Gospels to teach and inspire its readers. Others put a literal (word for word) interpretation on it. To Christian theologians, Satan (the Devil) is the chief demonic opponent to the will of God and goodness in humankind. The Hebrew word *satan* means "adversary or opponent."

Jesus Begins His Ministry

Jesus began his ministry when he was about

thirty years of age. He taught in the synagogues of Galilee, and he became well-known and very popular. Then Jesus went back to his home town of Nazareth. His teaching was rejected, and the townspeople of Nazareth wanted to kill him. However, Jesus was not harmed, and he left Nazareth.

Many People Healed

After arriving at the town of Capernaum, Jesus began preaching in the synagogue, where he healed a demon possessed man. (At this time, most sickness was believed to be caused by evil, unclean spirits called demons.) The news of what Jesus had done immediately spread throughout the area.

Soon the sick and disabled people of Capernaum

were being brought to Jesus, and he healed them. When Jesus left Capernaum to continue preaching his message in other cities, crowds of people tried to keep him from leaving them.

POSTSCRIPT. Emphasizing the power of the mind to heal may be the secret of Jesus' ability to bring about physical cures. Many sick people claim to be cured in faith-healing services or after visiting Lourdes and other shrines. The idea that people can help themselves through prayer and positive thinking is not uncommon.

Doctors are well aware of the healing effect a positive mental attitude can have on serious illnesses. So a doctor may prescribe a placebo (medicine with no active ingredient) to please or calm the patient. The *placebo effect* occurs when a patient is given a dummy pill and feels the same pain relief as when given a painkilling drug.

When patients expect to feel better or are told they will by their doctor or other authority figure, their conditions will likely improve. The healing power of the mind cannot be ignored.

News About Jesus Spreads

After leaving Capernaum, Jesus healed a leper and told him not to tell anyone. However, the news of the leper's healing spread quickly. Great crowds came to hear Jesus and to be healed of their illnesses. People came to Jesus from everywhere. Jesus could not enter a city publicly, and he had to stay out in the barren wastelands.

Summary Analysis

Jesus

After he was baptized, Jesus successfully taught at synagogues in Galilee and was very popular. However, he was rejected by the people in his home town of Nazareth. Jesus went to Capernaum. He preached in the synagogue and healed the sick. The people tried to keep him from leaving them. Jesus attracted large supportive crowds in other cities. He publicly taught and healed the sick and disabled that were brought to him.

Prayer

The Lord's Prayer was given as a model prayer by Jesus to the disciples. It's not showy and is to the

point, while being brief and not repetitious. Jesus'
model prayer is an ideal example of his teaching.
It's the principal prayer of Christians.

The Message

Matthew, one of the twelve disciples chosen by
Jesus to accompany him, was a tax collector. (None
of Jesus' disciples were from the religious sector.)
Tax collectors were religious outcasts, because they
collected taxes for the Romans and were
notoriously corrupt.

The Pharisees (a major religious sect) and the
scribes (experts in Jewish Mosaic law) complained
about Jesus associating with tax collectors and
other sinners. So Jesus told the parable, "The Lost
Sheep" to them.

Jesus' parable portrays God as being chiefly interested in the individual person----not in groups. The lesson of the parable is clear: **God wants every one----especially those he has lost.** This is a comforting message that brings hope to every man and woman. It was a startling new idea to religious groups, like the Pharisees and scribes.

Closing Thoughts

Today, the reality of God cannot be proved or disproved by scientific research or philosophical logic. Any belief in God ultimately rests upon one thing----faith. A faithful commitment to a higher power is practical and justified if it makes a *worthwhile* difference in the life of the believer.

Final Week

Jesus Enters Jerusalem

Jesus' popularity with the people was very evident when he entered Jerusalem riding on a young donkey, and large enthusiastic crowds greeted and praised him. Many spread their coats before Jesus and placed leafy branches along the way. A huge crowd of people took branches from palm trees and went to meet Jesus.

POSTSCRIPT. Palm Sunday observes Jesus' entry into Jerusalem. It comes one week before Easter.

Merchants Driven From the Temple

Jesus went to the Temple and drove out all the merchants who where conducting business in it. He told them they had turned the Temple into a den of thieves. Jesus began teaching daily in the Temple. He also healed the blind and crippled that came to him. The chief priests and other prominent leaders were angry, and they wanted to get rid of Jesus.

Judas Agrees to Betray Jesus

Judas Iscariot——one of the twelve disciples——met with the chief priests and agreed to hand Jesus over to them. The chief priests gave Judas thirty pieces of silver. Judas began looking for an opportunity to have Jesus arrested when there were no crowds of people around.

Eucharist Established

Jesus and the disciples shared a meal on the night before he was crucified. (It's called the Last Supper.) Jesus established the Eucharist when he solemnly shared bread and wine with them. Jesus instructed the disciples to continue this act in remembrance of him.

POSTSCRIPT. Christians have described the Eucharist in different ways including the Mass, Holy Communion, and the Lord's Supper. Christians also differ in their interpretation of this sacrament and in the manner and frequency of its observance.

In the sacrament of baptism Christians are immersed or showered in water in the name of the Father, Son, and Holy Spirit. Some Christians do not practice infant baptism. Others insist on immersion, and a few reject all external rites—including baptism.

Because the sacraments are so differently defined by the many Christian denominations, it is impossible to give a single, clear-cut explanation of them.

Jesus Arrested

At the Last Supper, Jesus told the disciples that one of them would betray him. Jesus indicated to Judas that he was the traitor, and Judas left immediately. After the meal, Jesus and the eleven remaining disciples went to a place called Gethsemane.

Jesus told the disciples that he was saddened to

the point of death. He withdrew a short distance from them and began to pray. (Clearly, Jesus was aware of the agony he would endure, because of the treacherous betrayal of Judas.)

Jesus returned to the disciples after praying, and Judas Iscariot arrived with a large armed group. Judas immediately greeted and kissed Jesus, as a signal to the others that he was the one to be arrested. Jesus was seized. The disciples left him and fled into the predawn darkness.

Jesus Before Caiaphas

Jesus was taken to the home of the High Priest Caiaphas, where a council of chief priests and other leaders had gathered. He was brought before this Jewish court. Witnesses gave false testimony against Jesus. However, he remained silent and would not answer his accusers.

Then Caiaphas, who presided over the trial, questioned Jesus. When Jesus responded, Caiaphas immediately declared him guilty of blasphemy for claiming to be the Messiah. Caiaphas declared, there was no further need for witnesses, and he asked the court for their verdict. The court condemned Jesus to death.

Peter Denies Jesus

When Jesus was arrested, he was taken to the high priest's home. Peter----one of the twelve disciples----followed far behind and into the courtyard. While in the courtyard, Peter passionately denied knowing Jesus three times.

Then Peter remembered Jesus' prediction of his triple denial, and he began to cry.

Precognition

Jesus' foretelling of Peter's triple denial is a memorable example of precognition----seeing into the future. However, there is evidence for precognition outside the Gospels. Have you suddenly, seriously thought about a friend or acquaintance that you haven't seen or heard from for a long time? Then you go to your mailbox and find a letter or you get a telephone call from that person. So called "coincidences" like these are not uncommon.

Mark Twain had a vivid dream that his brother had died, and he saw his brother's corpse laid out in a casket. Shortly after Twain's dream, his brother died in a tragic accident. When Mark Twain saw his brother's corpse, it was laid out exactly as it was in his dream. This event is recounted in Mark Twain's biography.

Clearly, precognition seems more than coincidental when it can be confirmed beyond the possibility of chance. For example, the Titanic disaster has provided the greatest number of authenticated cases of precognition for a single event. Many people experienced horrifyingly precise visions of it.

Jesus Before Pontius Pilate

After being condemned to death by a Jewish court, Jesus was brought to Pontius Pilate, the

Roman governor of Judea. (Judas regretted what he had done and committed suicide.) It was Pilate's custom to release any one prisoner the people wanted during the Passover celebration. So Pilate asked the crowd that had gathered before him which prisoner he should release to them---- Barabbas or Jesus.

Just then, Pilate received a message from his wife. Her message warned Pilate to have nothing to do with Jesus, because she had a terrible dream about him. Pilate also knew that religious leaders had arrested Jesus because of his popularity with the people, which they envied. In the meantime, the chief priests had stirred up the crowd to demand the release of Barabbas and for Jesus to be crucified.

Jesus Sentenced to Death

Pilate tried to release Jesus. When he saw a riot was starting, he washed his hands in front of the unruly crowd and disclaimed any responsibility for Jesus' death. Pilate told the angry mob they were responsible. The mob shouted back that the blood of Jesus would be on them and their children. Then Pilate released Barabbas. After Jesus was whipped, Pilate gave him to the Roman soldiers to crucify.

POSTSCRIPT. Cornelius Tacitus, first century Roman historian, recorded the sentence to death of Jesus by Pontius Pilate.

Premonitions

Many people, like Pilate's wife, have reported receiving premonitions via dreams or other means that have been authenticated. Shortly before his

assassination, President Abraham Lincoln had a

foreboding dream, which he described to credible

witnesses the following morning.

In his well-known dream, Lincoln saw a body

lying in state. Soldiers guarded it, and people were

sobbing and mourning. Lincoln asked a soldier,

whose body was lying there. He was told the

president was dead, killed by an assassin. President

Lincoln awoke.

Premonitions can also be vague, disturbing

feelings foretelling the future. For instance, a man

suddenly feels a fearful wave of sadness when his

daughter embarks on a trip that would end in her

death.

In many instances, premonitions seem to be more

than coincidental when connected to information that becomes known later. Following the Titanic disaster, many people came forward with canceled tickets and other supporting evidence to confirm their premonitions concerning the disaster.

Golgotha

After Pilate turned Jesus over to the soldiers, they made fun of Jesus. They beat and spat on Jesus, while they mocked him. The soldiers forced a man named Simon to carry Jesus' cross to the crucifixion site. The site was in a place called Golgotha from Hebrew *gulgoleth*, meaning "skull.".

POSTSCRIPT. Christians call the place where Jesus was crucified Calvary from Latin *calvaria*, meaning "a bare skull." The name of the area may have come from its appearance or its use as an execution site.

Crucifixion

Jesus was nailed to a cross at nine o'clock in the morning. A sign was placed above Jesus' cross designating him, "King of the Jews." Two robbers were also crucified with Jesus, one on his left and the other on his right. The Roman soldiers threw dice for Jesus' clothes. Religious leaders and people passing by mocked and ridiculed Jesus. Women from Galilee that came to Jerusalem with Jesus watched from a distance.

Jesus' mother, some women from Galilee, and "the disciple whom he loved" (usually identified as John) stood near Jesus' cross. It became dark from noon until about three o'clock when Jesus died, and the veil of the Temple was torn in two. It secluded the holiest place in the Temple.

POSTSCRIPT. Good Friday commemorates Jesus' death. It is observed the Friday before Easter Sunday.

Synchronicity

The mysterious afternoon darkness preceding Jesus' death and the tearing of the Temple veil when he died may be cited as examples of synchronicity.

The word *synchronicity* was originated by the eminent psychologist Carl Jung to describe meaningful coincidence that has no apparent cause. This concept is a theoretical approach to psychic phenomena.

Final Week

A chance meeting leading to a long term relationship or an unforeseen job opportunity are common examples of synchronicity. Miraculous events (including unexplainable cures and answered prayers) can also be classified as synchronistic experiences, because there is no apparent cause producing them. Instances of synchronicity point to the meaningful role seemingly chance events play in everyday life and a connection between coincidence and the paranormal.

Summary Analysis

Jesus

Jesus' popularity was evidenced by the growing multitudes of people that came to him from everywhere. So it is not surprising, huge crowds greeted Jesus when he entered Jerusalem. The city of Jerusalem was the focal point for the religious, business, and political establishments. By going to Jerusalem at the time of the Passover celebration, Jesus brought the challenge of his ministry directly to the very heart of the peoples' lives.

Religious Leaders

When Jesus expelled the merchants from the Temple and began teaching there, religious leaders were angry. Clearly, the Temple business community, to insure keeping their locations, made large donations to the Temple treasury on which religious leaders had become dependent.

In addition, Jesus was well-known and very popular. Many people began to follow him. Religious leaders were afraid they would lose their positions of leadership if Jesus' ministry was allowed to continue.

Jesus was arrested. He was taken to the home of the High Priest Caiaphas, who presided over a court that condemned Jesus to death. The chief priests and other leaders brought Jesus before the Roman Governor Pontius Pilate, who had sole authority for putting him to death.

Pontius Pilate

Pilate received a message on behalf of Jesus from his wife. He also knew Jesus' arrest and trial was set up by religious leaders. So he tried to release Jesus. However, the chief priests persuaded the people to demand the release of Barabbas and the crucifixion of Jesus.

Barabbas had been imprisoned for leading a rebellion against Pilate's government in Jerusalem and for murder. There had also been a massacre of Jews at the Temple in Jerusalem, ordered by Pilate. Politically motivated, Pilate undoubtedly realized another public disturbance would reflect on his ability to govern and could result in his removal from office. So when Pilate saw an angry mob was starting to riot, he released Barabbas and handed

Jesus over to be crucified by the Roman soldiers.

POSTSCRIPT. In 36 A.D., public outrage over Pilate's behavior resulted in his removal from office.

NOTE: Obviously, the personal guilt of Jewish religious leaders and the riotous mob, who played a major part in bringing about Jesus' crucifixion, cannot be charged to all Jewish people.

Closing Thoughts

Jesus' followers came to believe, God was acting through him. In Jesus, they saw the dawning of a new age. But their hopes were dashed by his crucifixion. Then came the Resurrection, a stunning event that required a new assessment of what Jesus was all about.

Resurrection

Burial of Jesus

Joseph of Arimathea was a follower of Jesus. He asked Pilate for Jesus' body, and Pilate released it to him. Joseph wrapped the body in a clean linen cloth and placed it in a tomb cut out of the rock. It was Joseph's new tomb. Before leaving, Joseph rolled a large stone across the entrance of the tomb.

Guards Placed at the Tomb

The day after Jesus' burial, the chief priests and

Pharisees obtained Pilate's permission to place guards at the tomb. They sealed the large stone that blocked the entrance and posted guards to secure the tomb. This was done so Jesus' disciples could not steal his body and say that he had risen from the dead.

Faithful Women

Faithful women traveled throughout Galilee with Jesus. Many of them also gave from their personal means to support Jesus and the twelve disciples.

When the body of Jesus was taken down from the cross, the Galilean women that had come to Jerusalem with him followed and saw it carried into the tomb. The women went home and prepared spices and ointments to embalm Jesus' body.

Early Sunday morning, the women went to the tomb. The large stone covering the entrance had been rolled aside. When they entered, they did not find Jesus' body. Two men, dressed in shining robes, told the women that Jesus was alive. The women hurried to tell Jesus' disciples what had happened.

POSTSCRIPT. Easter Sunday is one week after Palm Sunday. It commemorates Jesus' Resurrection.

Report of the Guards

The guards reported they had fallen asleep during the night, and Jesus' disciples had stolen his body. The Gospels indicate, the guards were bribed, told what to say, and assured they would be kept out of trouble by the chief priests and other leaders.

POSTSCRIPT. The guards could have been put to death for sleeping while on watch. If the guards were asleep, how could they have known Jesus' disciples had stolen his body? No one was ever arrested or tried for stealing the body of Jesus, and a "stolen body" was never found.

The Disciples

Jesus chose twelve disciples to accompany him. He was betrayed by Judas. The other disciples frightfully fled when Jesus was arrested. Peter passionately denied knowing him. When Jesus' body was taken down from the cross and laid in the tomb, none of the disciples were there. The women reported the empty tomb and what had happened, but the disciples didn't believe them.

Resurrection

Thomas would not believe unless he saw the nail wounds in Jesus' hands, put his fingers into them, and placed his hand in Jesus' side. (A Roman soldier pierced Jesus' side with a spear after Jesus died and was still on the cross.)

Summary Analysis

Some Conclusions

Faithful women remained dedicated to Jesus and never wavered in their devotion to him. Jesus' disciples became fearful skeptics. Then an astonishing thing happened. The disciples bravely and sincerely began preaching Jesus' Resurrection. They endured persecution and martyrs deaths, rather than deny their faith. These facts make it hard to believe the disciples had stolen Jesus' body.

Closing Thoughts

The change that came into the lives of Jesus' disciples strongly suggests they really believed Jesus had risen from the dead. It also suggests,

Resurrection

Jesus' doubting disciples----especially Thomas----

had eye witnessed convincing proof of his

Resurrection and the existence of an afterlife.

Afterlife

Near Death Experiences

Like Jesus' disciples, contemporary men and
women also want convincing proof of the existence
of an afterlife. True experiences of people, who
were declared clinically dead and been revived,
point to the beginning of a transition to an afterlife.
Research of this phenomenon by Elisabeth
Kubler-Ross, M.D. and other scientists has provided
strong support for human survival of bodily death.

Contact Between Living Minds

The direct transference of thoughts from one person to another without using the usual sensory channels, like sight or hearing, is an example of extrasensory perception (ESP).

Dr. Joseph Banks Rhine coined the term *ESP* and popularized it. Dr. Rhine founded the first parapsychology laboratory in the United States at Duke University in Durham, North Carolina. Experiments at this laboratory, using statistical analyses, provided supporting evidence for extrasensory communication between living minds.

POSTSCRIPT. Parapsychological experiments have provided millions to one odds against chance----the scientific standard.

Contact Between Deceased and Living Minds

Today, the Greek letter *psi* is the general term used by parapsychologists to name ESP and other psychic phenomena dealing with the human mind. Numerous cases of psi communication have been investigated in which it appears a deceased person's mind (consciousness) contacts a living person's mind via an apparition, dream, or other means.

IMPORTANT: There are cases of psi communication in which it appears a deceased person's mind conveys previously unknown information (later, found to be true) to a living person's mind. The following cases have been researched and validated. They provide strong support for human survival of bodily death.

An Obsolete Form of Shorthand

A few weeks after her husband's death, a widowed mother noticed her four year old son scribbling on some paper. The child gave the scribbling to his mother. Because the writing looked like shorthand, the mother showed it to a public stenographer. The stenographer indicated the writing was an obsolete form of shorthand, but she was able to translate it.

The translated message began with an affectionate expression the widow's husband used especially for her. Then it revealed the location of insurance policies and other valuable papers in a safe deposit box of a bank. The discovery of the documents cleared up the monetary problems that had been caused by the death of the widow's husband.

POSTSCRIPT. At one time, the widow's husband was a stenographer. He had used the same obsolete form of shorthand that his four year old son used to write the message.

The R101

The British dirigible R101 crashed, exploded, and burned on October 5, 1930. Forty-five of her crew, including Flight Lieutenant H. C. Irwin, were killed. Two days after the crash, Eileen Garrett (a medium) went into a trance. In the voice of a man, who identified himself as Flight Lieutenant Irwin, she told what had caused the crash in technical terms only an airman would know.

POSTSCRIPT. The final reports on the cause of the

crash verified the truthfulness of the words spoken

in the trance.

Summary Analysis

Closing Thoughts

We live in a world filled with psychic phenomena pointing to the survival of the human mind and individual consciousness, which continues to live on after bodily death. In certain situations it can make its presence known to us. There are no ultimate answers, and most of us have had our doubts. However, there is compelling evidence for what men and women have believed for thousands of years----there is life *after* life.

Vignettes

The Monkey and Me

I sat before a typewriter working on time consuming research for my book, and I wondered if I would be able to complete it.

I grinned when I remembered an article I had read. It stated that if an immortal monkey was set before a typewriter for an unlimited time, the monkey by chance would eventually produce Shakespeare's *Hamlet*.

Vignettes

I casually thought about the monkey and me. The monkey was immortal and had unlimited time. I was eighty years old, not immortal, and didn't have unlimited time. Then I remembered that by chance the monkey would eventually produce _Hamlet_. I smiled and began writing very short stories----vignettes----hoping that by chance I would eventually complete my book.

Number Phenomena

I've always been interested in the possible relationship between numbers and a person's destiny. So one day I decided to record my numbers. I awoke at 10:00 A.M. It was the 10th day of the month, and I made out a check for 10 dollars to my favorite charity.

As I was walking to the market, I found a 10 dollar bill on the ground. At the market, I purchased a 10 dollar lottery ticket that had a 10 million dollar jackpot. I returned the next day and found out I had won 10 dollars.

I collected my 10 dollars, and I realized that number phenomena comes together in ways that are unexpected, unpredictable, and usually unnoticed.

Unidentified Flying Objects

Years ago, I attended a conference about the UFO controversy. It took place at the convention center in Anaheim, California. At the conference, I met

Betty Hill, and I became interested in abduction cases.

Betty Hill and her husband, Barney, were abducted by occupants of a UFO while driving home on a highway through the mountains. The couple remembered the incident after deep hypnosis. Both of them were examined aboard the UFO. Betty had a long needle inserted into her navel, and she was told it was a pregnancy test. This test (amniocentesis) was unknown to doctors at that time. The couple was told they would forget the incident, and they were taken back to their car.

While hypnotized, Betty drew a star map that she had seen in the UFO. Years later, the pattern of stars on Betty's map was found, and its basic star system was identified as Zeta Reticuli. Today, this system is believed to be capable of supporting life.

I visited Kitt Peak National Observatory, located outside Tucson, Arizona. I learned the observatory has a 36-foot-diameter radio telescope. Also, the search for extraterrestrial intelligence (*SETI*) outside the solar system is being carried out with radio telescopes. This type of telescope could detect radio signals sent by intelligent life on planets in distant star systems.

Four spacecraft (Pioneer 10 and 11, Voyagers 1 and 2) are heading toward outer space. They contain engraved plaques and recorded messages of words and music from Earth that by chance another civilization might find.

Classic abduction cases, like that of Betty and Barney Hill, point to the existence of extraterrestrials (*ETS*). Radio telescopes and the Pioneer and Voyager missions are currently searching for ETS.

The SETI League is an organization searching for extraterrestrial intelligence. Its microwave Project Argus was started without government financing or equipment. When completed, it will watch and listen across the entire sky.

What should you do? Your best option is called *watchful waiting.* It doesn't mean that you do nothing. It means that you wait and see.

Reincarnation

The best evidence for reincarnation has come from cases in which a living person has past life memories of a deceased person that can be traced and verified by credible witnesses and indisputable proof. Behavior and physical similarities between the deceased and the living person may be present. The living person may experience *deja vu, the* feeling of familiarity with a place or situation he or she has never been in before.

Many accept the presence of reincarnation in nature and humanity. In nature, morning and evening are followed by morning again. In the same way, human birth and death are followed by rebirth. Reincarnation can't be easily dismissed.

Men and women have believed for thousands of years----there is life before life.

The Lost Dutchman Mine

The legendary Lost Dutchman Mine contains a rich deposit of gold, so loose it can be scooped up in your hands. It is located outside Phoenix, Arizona in the Superstition Mountains. The Dutchman was a German prospector named Jacob Waltz. He died in 1891 at 81 years of age. Several people claimed they saw gold ore that Waltz said he got from a mine in the Superstition Mountains. Locals searched for the mine and failed to find it.

Years later, the legend began. The mystery of the Lost Dutchman Mine received extensive media coverage. Many books were published on it, and Hollywood released a movie about it. Men and women from all over the world came to search for the mine.

Vignettes

In fact, I went to Arizona to search for the Lost Dutchman Mine. I went into the Superstition Mountains at the First Water entrance. Of course, I didn't find the mine. Still many people have told stories of finding it. However, if the Lost Dutchman Mine was really found, treasure hunters wouldn't believe it. They'd continue searching for the mine and its gold. .

I understand why my fellow treasure hunters---- whether searching for gold, love, or God---- are so doggedly persistent. An old prospector told me this: "Searching for a treasure is the next best thing to finding it."

Summary Analysis

Closing Thoughts

I hope my book has provided guidelines in areas,
like psychic phenomena and UFOs, where there are
no clear-cut answers. I've done my best to give
accurate information without interpreting it
according to a particular belief or opinion.

Appendix

Growing Old

A man and his wife were going through an old family picture album and remembering some good times. However, they were heavyhearted when they looked at pictures of themselves and remembered their passed youth. The man and his wife were over eighty years old. Both of them had arthritis, and they were struggling with other age

age related illnesses. The couple also had trouble

passing the vision tests for their drivers' licenses.

This man and woman wanted to do something

that would help them cope with growing old. So the

couple flew to a famous five star hotel and made first

class reservations on a luxurious cruise ship.

Living well may not be enough, but it sure helps.

Peace of Mind

A young man told a wise old man the following:

"Life isn't always fair. Being good frequently fails to

pay off, and there's no special reason why I've

lost out on certain things."

The wise old man answered as follows: "You will

find peace of mind only when you stop questioning

the uncertainty of life and you start appreciating the good fortune you still have."

The young man drove to his modest little home. It was just right for two. Then the young man and his wife shared a casual meal on the back patio. After watching a long lasting sunset, they went to bed. Life was good.

The young man realized the wise old man was right. Now, the young man treasured the good fortune he still possessed, and he stopped worrying about the things he had lost out on.

Men and Women

I wondered if there was anything *all* men and women really have in common. Most men like sports and cars. Most women like shopping and clothes. Of course, men and women usually have different ideas about love, sex, and marriage.

I visited a married couple. The husband told me his wife was hopelessly demanding. He complained about her always shopping and waiting outside dress stores for her.

The wife told me her husband was asking for too much. She complained about him always watching sports on TV and waiting for him to stop messing around with cars.

Now, I understood what *all* men and women really have in common. More than anything else, they want to get their own way.

Family

It was the day after Thanksgiving, and I was examining the decorations that I traditionally put up for Christmas. I told my wife, I wouldn't be decorating our home for Christmas. Then I reminded her that we were alone, and none of our children or grandchildren would be with us.

My wife and I reminisced about our children, grandchildren, and Christmas past. We remembered, my wife's uncle was going to be Santa Claus at a Christmas party. So on his way to the party, he stopped by our home dressed as Santa Claus and thrilled our three young children.

We also recalled taking our charmingly, naive granddaughter on her first visit to see Santa Claus at a local department store.

Then we remembered the Christmas day our innocent baby great granddaughter, after opening her presents, looked into the fireplace chimney. She was trying to find Santa Claus.

Now I realized, my wife and I were not alone. Memories of our children and grandchildren would always be with us.

I began decorating our home for Christmas.

Finding Love

Shakespeare's Othello grieved that he did not love wisely, but too well. Many present-day men and women also wish they had loved wisely and not too well, but this isn't love.

Love is never wise hearted or moderate. You

never know where or when you will find love or whether you will keep it or lose it. Intuition can keep love; reasoning can lose it. Sometimes you throw love away. The only thing sure is that you're never sure.

Shakespeare and I would be the first to tell you---- you just might find love today.

When Love Is Done

A husband was terminally ill in the hospital, and his wife was at his bedside. Arrangements were being made to move him to a hospice. The caring wife felt so much love, but she was afraid that when her husband passed the love would be done. She whispered, "I love you," and kissed her husband.

Appendix

The tearful wife stayed with her husband. She
could do nothing to stop his pain, but she was
unwilling to let him suffer alone. When her
husband passed, she would not leave him. She had
never felt the presence of love so strongly.

Now this dear wife understood: love is never
done----love is forever.

Written by Francis William Bourdillon, this poem
touched my heart:

> The night has a thousand eyes,
> And the day but one;
> Yet the light of the bright world dies
> With the dying of the sun.
>
> The mind has a thousand eyes,
> And the heart but one;
> Yet the light of a whole life dies
> When love is done.

Author's Note

In these pages, I've recorded my feelings and
beliefs to pass down to others, especially loved ones.
I want to leave something more than my money
behind.

About the Author

Michael Zyvant is a businessman that retired in the southwest and turned author. Michael and his wife live in a little hilltop house, loving their view of mountains and sunsets.

Short Index for the Life of Jesus

Short Index for the Paranormal